# INSECT WORLD
# STICK INSECTS

SANDRA MARKLE

MASTERS OF DEFENSE

LERNER PUBLICATIONS COMPANY  MINNEAPOLIS

# FOR CURIOUS KIDS EVERYWHERE

## ACKNOWLEDGMENTS
The author would like to thank Dr. Juergen Berger, Max-Planck Institute for Developmental Biology, Tubingen, Germany, and Paul D. Brock, Phasmid Study Group, Great Britain, for sharing their expertise and enthusiasm. The author would also like to thank Dr. Simon Pollard, Curator of Invertebrate Zoology at Canterbury Museum, Christchurch, New Zealand, for his help with the scientific name pronunciation guides. Finally, a special thanks to Skip Jeffery, who shared the effort and joy of creating this book.

Lerner Publications Company
A division of Lerner Publishing Group, Inc.
241 First Avenue North
Minneapolis, MN 55401

Website address: www.lernerbooks.com

Library of Congress Cataloging-in-Publication Data

Markle, Sandra.
     Stick Insects: masters of defense / by Sandra Markle.
        p.   cm. — (Insect world)
     Includes bibliographical references and index.
      ISBN 978–0–8225–7296–1 (lib. bdg. : alk. paper)
       1. Stick insects—Juvenile literature.  I. Title.
  QL509.5.M37  2008
  595.7'27—dc22               2007025268

Manufactured in the United States of America
1 2 3 4 5 6 – DP – 13 12 11 10 09 08

# CONTENTS

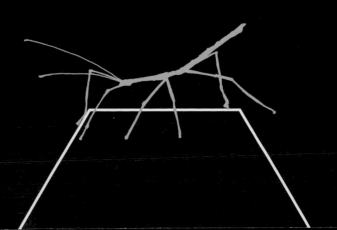

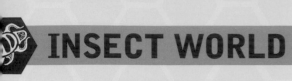
## WELCOME TO THE WORLD OF INSECTS—

those animals nicknamed bugs. It truly is the insects' world. Scientists have discovered more than a million kinds—more than any other kind of animal. And they are everywhere— even on the frozen continent of Antarctica.

So how can you tell if an animal is an insect rather than a spider *(right)*? Both belong to a group of animals called arthropods (AR-throh-podz). The animals in this group share some features. They have bodies divided into segments, jointed legs, and a stiff exoskeleton. This is a skeleton on the outside, like a suit of armor. But the one sure way to tell if an animal is an insect is to count its legs. All adult insects have six legs, and they're the only animals in the world with six legs.

This book is about stick insects. These insects have amazing ways to defend, or protect, themselves against insect-eating predators.

Like all insects, a stick insect's body temperature rises and falls with the temperature around it. So it must warm up to be active.

## ON THE OUTSIDE

Take a look at this adult female Costa Rican stick insect. Its body feels like tough plastic. Instead of having a hard, bony skeleton inside the way you do, an insect has an exoskeleton. This hard coat covers its whole body—even its eyes. The exoskeleton is made up of separate plates connected by stretchy tissue. This lets the insect bend and move. Check out the other key parts that all stick insects share.

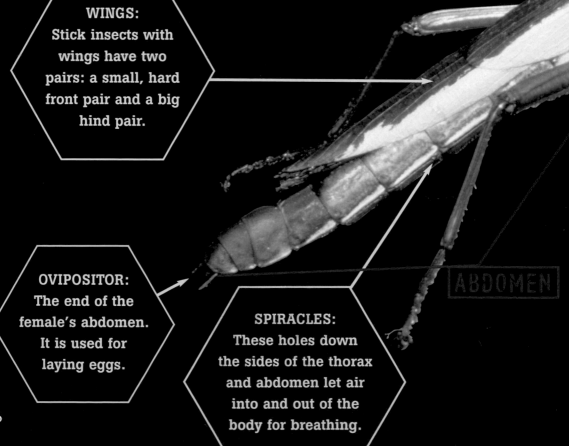

**WINGS:**
Stick insects with wings have two pairs: a small, hard front pair and a big hind pair.

**OVIPOSITOR:**
The end of the female's abdomen. It is used for laying eggs.

**SPIRACLES:**
These holes down the sides of the thorax and abdomen let air into and out of the body for breathing.

ABDOMEN

6

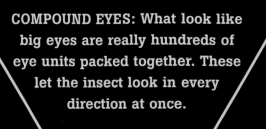

**COMPOUND EYES:** What look like big eyes are really hundreds of eye units packed together. These let the insect look in every direction at once.

**ANTENNA:** This is one of a pair of movable feelers. Hairs on the antennae detect chemicals for taste and smell.

HEAD

**MANDIBLES:** These are hard, toothlike jaws on the outside of the mouth. They are used to bite and grind.

THORAX

STICK INSECT FACT

**LEGS AND FEET:** These are used for walking and holding on. All legs are attached to the thorax.

Not all kinds of adult stick insects have wings. Those that have wings usually also have simple eyes between their compound eyes. These eyes sense light from dark and help stick insects find their way in flight.

**Look inside an adult female stick insect.**

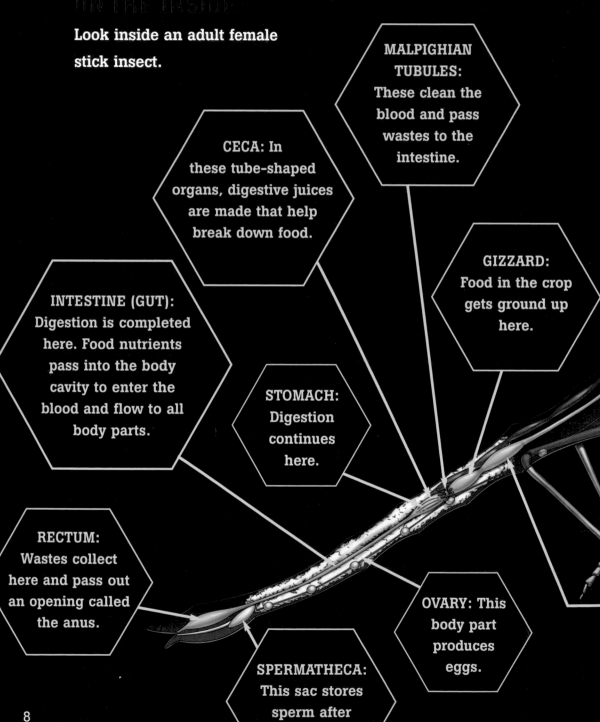

MALPIGHIAN TUBULES: These clean the blood and pass wastes to the intestine.

CECA: In these tube-shaped organs, digestive juices are made that help break down food.

GIZZARD: Food in the crop gets ground up here.

INTESTINE (GUT): Digestion is completed here. Food nutrients pass into the body cavity to enter the blood and flow to all body parts.

STOMACH: Digestion continues here.

RECTUM: Wastes collect here and pass out an opening called the anus.

OVARY: This body part produces eggs.

SPERMATHECA: This sac stores sperm after mating.

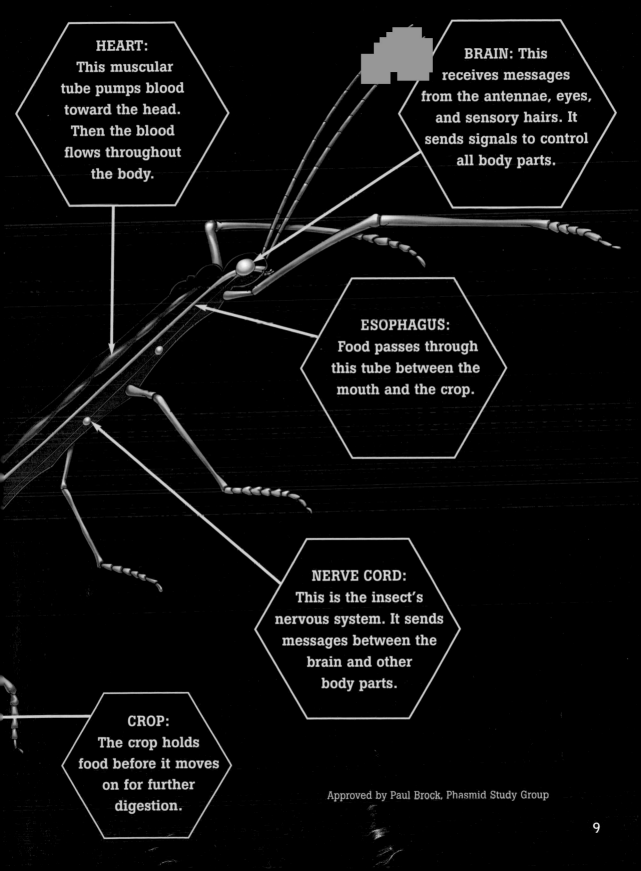

**HEART:**
This muscular tube pumps blood toward the head. Then the blood flows throughout the body.

**BRAIN:** This receives messages from the antennae, eyes, and sensory hairs. It sends signals to control all body parts.

**ESOPHAGUS:**
Food passes through this tube between the mouth and the crop.

**NERVE CORD:**
This is the insect's nervous system. It sends messages between the brain and other body parts.

**CROP:**
The crop holds food before it moves on for further digestion.

Approved by Paul Brock, Phasmid Study Group

# BECOMING AN ADULT

Insect babies grow into being adults in two ways: complete metamorphosis (me-teh-MOR-feh-sus) and incomplete metamorphosis. Metamorphosis means change. Stick insects develop through incomplete metamorphosis. Their life includes three stages: egg, nymph, and adult. The nymphs look and act much like small adults. But nymphs can't reproduce. Compare this stick insect nymph to the adult. The nymphs of adults with wings lack fully developed wings.

IN COMPLETE METAMORPHOSIS, insects go through four stages: egg, larva, pupa, and adult. Each stage looks and behaves very differently.

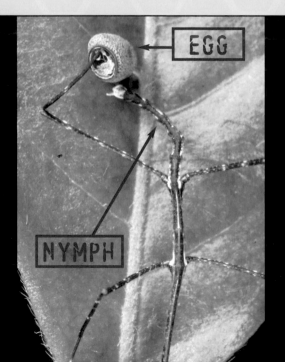

EGG

NYMPH

ADULT

A stick insect is a master at staying safe. This Australian stick insect's body is colored and shaped to blend in with the plants it eats. Other kinds of stick insects also have other ways to defend themselves. Some are able to make a quick escape. Others are able to play tricks that scare away predators. Still others are able to attack and fight back. Some are simply too big a mouthful for most insect-eating predators.

# BUILT TO HIDE

Stick insects are naturally camouflaged. This means they blend in with their surroundings. Their coloring and even their shape look like the plants on which they live and feed. Some, like this Costa Rican stick insect, have extra bits to add to their disguise. Flaky parts stick out of this stick insect's exoskeleton. That makes it look like it's covered with small plants. It blends in perfectly with the tree limbs it calls home.

STICK INSECT FACT

While a stick insect is resting, it often holds its antennae between its outstretched front legs. This helps it look more like a stick.

About 20 kinds of stick insects in Asia have a special disguise. They have extra parts that make them look like leaves. If there is a breeze blowing, these stick insects sway like the leaves around them. Sometimes one leaf insect bites another one thinking it is food.

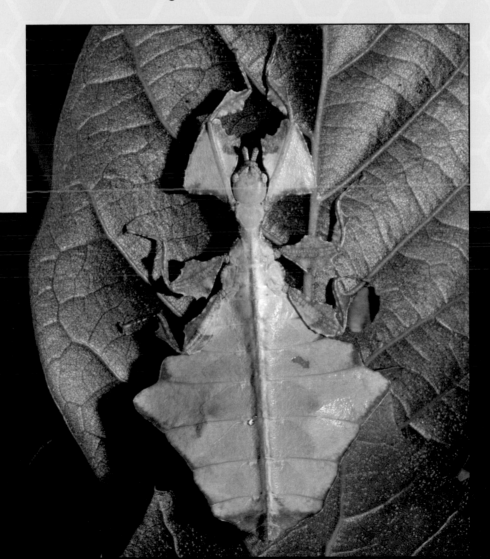

## COVERING THEIR TRACKS

A stick insect uses its mouthparts to hold and move the leaf it eats. The insect turns its head as it chews. This makes a hole in the leaf.

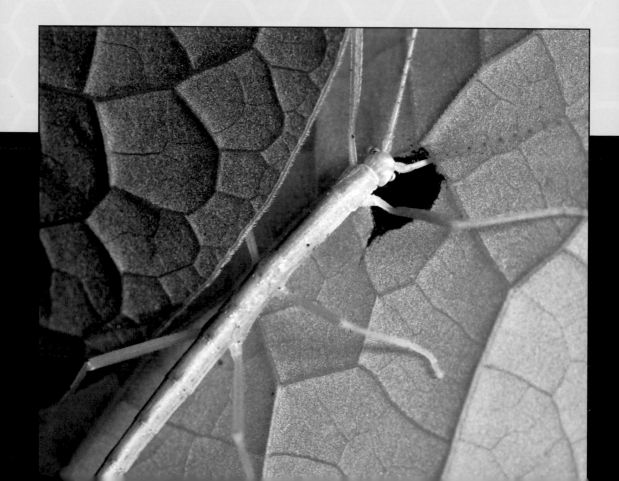

A predator might spot the leaves with holes. Then it might find the stick insect. To keep that from happening, stick insects will eat the whole leaf, if it's a small one. Or they will move away from the holes in a larger leaf before settling down to rest.

**STICK INSECT FACT**

Stick insects usually move to a new feeding site at night. Predators are less likely to see them moving in the dark.

Eating a lot of leaves means stick insects produce a lot of wastes. Piles of wastes could attract predators. That's another reason stick insects leave an eating site before they rest. At rest, this Madagascar stick insect hangs onto a branch and stretches out. It tries to look like the twigs around it. If an enemy comes close, the stick insect holds its legs against its body and drops to the ground. It hides in the fallen leaves. The stick insect is likely to stay hidden on the ground until dark. Then it climbs back up the tree to continue its meal.

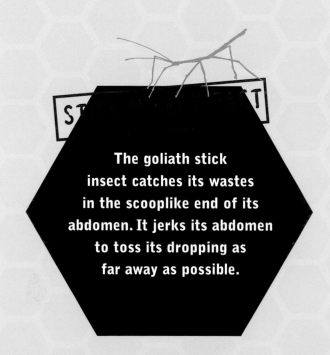

The goliath stick insect catches its wastes in the scooplike end of its abdomen. It jerks its abdomen to toss its dropping as far away as possible.

# BREAKING FREE

If a predator grabs a stick insect by one of its long legs, the insect can still escape. Stick insects can break off their legs at the joint closest to the thorax. The insect loses a limb but saves its life. If a stick insect loses a leg as an adult, the leg won't grow back. If a nymph loses a leg, it will partly grow back.

Like adults, stick insect nymphs have an exoskeleton. As the nymph eats and grows, its exoskeleton becomes tight. The nymph *(right)* is molting, or shedding, its armorlike covering. Its exoskeleton split open along the back, and the nymph is pulling itself out. It is already covered by a new exoskeleton. That coat is soft at first. The nymph will hide by staying still until its exoskeleton hardens. If a nymph loses a leg, some of it grows back each time it molts. Nymphs molt five to six times before becoming adults.

**Nymphs often eat their skin after molting. This is yet another source of food energy.**

## PLAYING TRICKS

Some predators have sharp senses. These senses help them track down stick insects even though they are well disguised. This Asian stick insect has another way to save itself. If a predator comes close, the Asian stick insect opens its wings. It flashes its brightly colored stripes. This may scare the predator away. Or at least, it might startle the predator. This will give the stick insect enough time to glide away to safety.

**STICK INSECT FACT**

**Stick insects have claw tips on their feet. They can hang upside down from a branch, and this helps them hide too.**

When threatened, the Australian giant prickly stick insect curls its abdomen over its back. It doesn't really have a stinger, but it looks ready to strike with one. If this threat doesn't work, the male gives off a scented spray. People say this scent smells like peanut butter. Still, it drives off most insect–eating predators.

Females don't have a spray to fight off enemies. Most stick insect females are bigger than males. So the large female Australian giant's fake stinger seems an even bigger threat. That's usually enough to make predators avoid her.

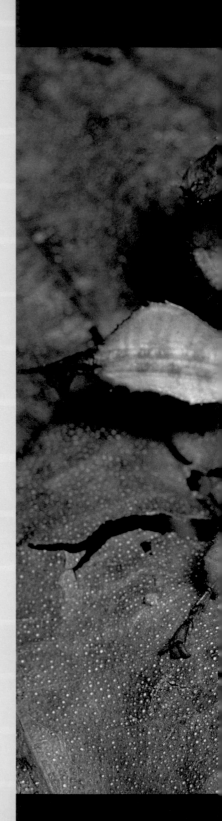

## STICKING UP FOR YOURSELF

A Panama rain forest stick insect stays safe by being armed. Its exoskeleton has sharp, spiky edges, or barbs, on its back. Whenever this stick insect isn't moving, it presses its belly against the branch it is on. That way, a predator only sees its armed back. The barbs are bright red, so predators will be sure to notice them.

Any predator that bites one of these stick insects will get a mouthful of sharp barbs. The predator is then likely to let go of its prickly stick-insect prey. The stick insect stays safe. The predator probably will leave other barbed stick insects alone too. This helps other prickly stick insects stay alive.

**STICK INSECT FACT**

Goliath stick insects have spiny legs. They will kick at a predator that comes too close.

This Papua New Guinea stick insect has hard, thornlike barbs all over its body. Each of its hind legs has a long spur. This stick insect stays alert, watching for predators with its big eyes. When a predator comes close, the stick insect lifts its rear end and hind legs. If it is attacked, the stick insect jerks its body to stab at its enemy. This usually makes the predator pull back. Then the stick insect holds its legs against its body and drops to the ground. Looking like a thorny twig, it stays safe hidden among the twigs and leaves. After dark, it climbs back up the tree and continues eating.

STICK INSECT FACT

If attacked, the Australian peppermint stick insect squirts out a blast of liquid from glands between its head and thorax. People say the spray smells like peppermint. But predators stay away.

The Peruvian fire stick is brightly colored all over. Its color is a warning to leave it alone. If a predator comes close, this stick insect shoots out a white liquid. This liquid comes from an opening behind its head. Fire sticks have been recorded squirting this liquid as far as 15 inches (38 centimeters). The liquid smells so bad that it drives most predators away. Fire stick nymphs hatch already armed. From the start, they are able to fire their liquid to defend themselves.

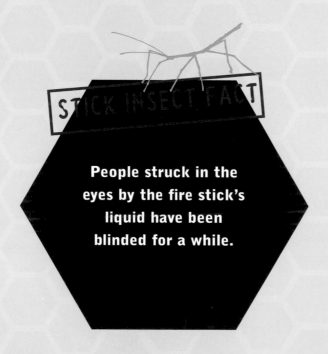

STICK INSECT FACT

People struck in the eyes by the fire stick's liquid have been blinded for a while.

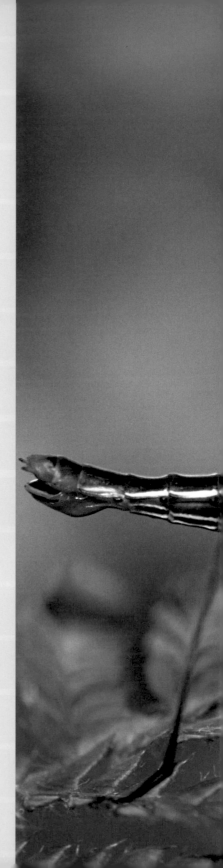

## TOO BIG TO BITE

This stick insect, which lives in Malaysia's rain forests, has yet another way to keep from being eaten. It quickly grows to be super big. In just four months, this stick insect goes from being 0.15 inches (0.39 cm) long inside its egg to an adult 13 inches (33 cm) long. It is too big a mouthful for many insect-eating predators, such as spiders and small lizards. Some kinds of stick insects are the world's longest insects.

All the real giant stick insects are females. Females need to be bigger than males to hold all the eggs they produce. They need to be bigger to be able to eat and digest lots of food too. They need extra food for energy to produce all those eggs.

STICK INSECT FACT

Females of a kind of Asian stick insect are the longest kind. They are as much as 13 inches (33 cm) long.

# LOTS OF EGGS

Producing lots of young is another kind of defense. Hundreds of babies mean that some will survive being eaten by predators. This helps stick insects as a whole to survive. But stick insects are so well camouflaged that finding a mate can be hard. They can't see one another easily, but they can sense one another. Female stick insects produce special scents called pheromones (FER-uh-mohnz). The males have sensory hairs on their antennae to track this scent. This Florida two-stripe walking stick male followed the female's pheromone trail. During mating, he transfers a packet of sperm, or male reproductive cells, to her body. He will die shortly after mating.

The female keeps on eating while eggs develop inside her. Then one night, she climbs down from her feeding tree. She pokes a hole into the ground with her tail end. She lays eggs in this hole. The female does this every few days until she has laid hundreds of eggs. Then she dies too. Most stick insects live about a year.

## STICK INSECT FACT

Some kinds of female stick insects, like Indian stick insects, are able to produce eggs without mating. This kind of reproduction is called parthenogenesis (par-theh-noh-JE-neh-sehs).

Stick insects produce hundreds of eggs. This usually means some eggs will survive to hatch even if predators eat others. Some stick insects, like the Florida two-striped, lay them in holes in the ground. Some glue their eggs to the underside of a leaf to hide them. Others just flick them away, one at a time. These eggs drop to the ground and are hard to find. This is because many kinds of stick insect eggs are also camouflaged. The eggs are the same color and shape as the seeds of the plant that is the stick insect's usual home.

One kind of
Thailand stick insect
holds the egg-laying record.
Each female produces
about 700 eggs.

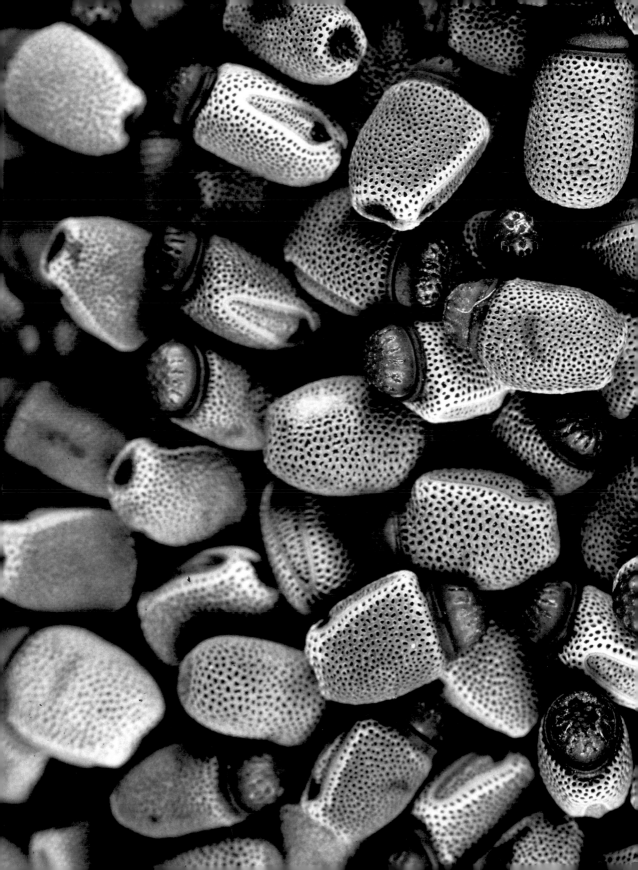

One Australian stick insect has developed a special way to protect its eggs. Each egg has a cap filled with a special food. The smell of this rich food attracts ants. The ants pick up the eggs, one by one, and carry them back to their nest. In the nest, the ants eat the egg caps. They put the eggs in the nest's garbage dump. Being in the ants' dump doesn't harm the eggs. The ants guard their nest against enemies, such as some kinds of insects and spiders. Being in the ants' nest protects the stick insect's eggs too. When the stick insect nymphs hatch, they crawl out of the nest. Then they go in search of a leafy meal.

**Some kinds of female wasps search for stick insect eggs. They inject them with their own eggs. The wasps' young hatch and grow up eating the baby stick insects inside the eggs.**

As soon as this Panama stick insect nymph hatched, it stretched out along a leaf. Its color and shape allow it to blend in perfectly. Hidden from predators, the nymph waits until night to start to eat. This nymph will survive to become an adult. It will mate and produce young. It will stay alive to carry on for another generation. This is, after all, the reason stick insects are masters of defense.

# STICK INSECTS AND OTHER INSECT MASTERS OF DEFENSE

STICK INSECTS BELONG TO A GROUP, or order, of insects called Phasmatodea (fas-ma-TOE-dee-ah). That name comes from the Greek word *phasma*, meaning "phantom." It describes how well stick insects can blend in and hide. There are more than 3,000 different kinds of stick insects.

SCIENTISTS GROUP LIVING and extinct animals with others that are similar. So stick insects are classified this way:

> Kingdom: Animalia
> Phylum: Arthropoda
> Class: Insecta
> Order: Phasmatodea

HELPFUL OR HARMFUL? Stick insects eat plant leaves, so they can harm plants. There are usually too few stick insects on a plant to do much damage, though. Young stick insects are helpful because there are lots of them. They are a source of food for insect-eating predators.

HOW BIG ARE stick insects? The northern walking stick *(outline below)* can be up to 4 inches (about 10 cm) long. Some grow up to 13 inches (33 cm) long. They are the world's longest insect.

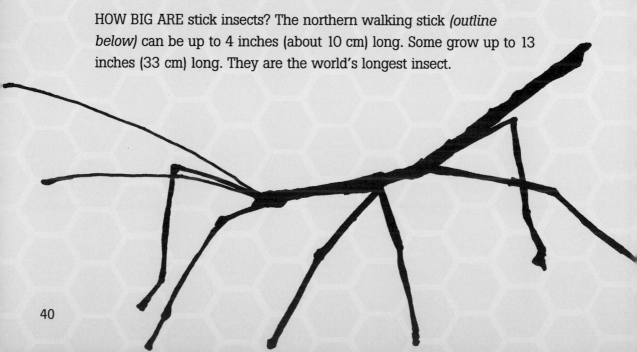

# MORE INSECT MASTERS OF DEFENSE

Other insects also have ways to defend themselves against predators. Compare these insect defenses to those used by stick insects.

**Bombardier beetles** have a chemical weapon to defend themselves. If attacked, a bombardier beetle twists its rear end toward its enemy. Then it shoots out two chemicals. The two chemicals mix together in the air. They form a smelly, boiling-hot liquid. The bombardier beetle, like all beetles, can't open its hard front wings fast enough to escape quickly. It counts on its spray to drive away ants and other predators.

**Spittle bugs** are a kind of plant-sucking insect. They hide while they eat by whipping up a mass of bubbles. This mass is called spittle, but it is really sticky goo that comes out of the bug's rear end. The spittle bug wiggles its tail end up and down to whip the goo into bubbles. Then it uses its hind legs to push the bubbles around its body. This mass of bubbles keeps predators from noticing it. The bubbles also keep the spittle bug from drying out.

**Click beetles** get their name from the noise they make while defending themselves. If grabbed by a predator, the click beetle bends its head and the front part of its thorax backward. Then it straightens out with a snapping motion. This makes a loud click and sends the beetle into the air. This move lets the click beetle make a quick getaway. It may take flight while in midair, or it may drop back to the ground. On the ground, the click beetle tucks its legs and antennae tight against its body. It stays still as though it were dead. With any luck, the predator will leave it alone.

# GLOSSARY

**abdomen:** the tail end of an insect. It contains systems for digestion and reproduction.

**adult:** the final stage of an insect's life cycle

**antennae:** movable, jointed parts on the insect's head used for sensing

**brain:** the body part that receives messages from the antennae, eyes, and sensory hairs. It sends signals to control all body parts.

**ceca** (SEE-ka)**:** tubes where digestive juices are made that help break down food

**complete metamorphosis:** a process of development in which the young looks and behaves very differently from the adult. Stages include egg, larva, pupa, and adult.

**compound eyes:** eyes that are really hundreds of eye units packed together. These let the insect look in every direction at once.

**crop:** area of the digestive system where food is held before it is passed on for further digestion

**defense:** a way to prevent attack

**egg:** a female reproductive cell; also the name given to the first stage of an insect's life cycle

**esophagus** (eh-SAH-feh-gus)**:** a tube through which food passes from the mouth to the crop, or stomach

**exoskeleton:** protective, skeleton-like covering on the outside of the body

**gizzard:** body part where food stored in the crop begins to be ground up

**head:** the insect's body part that has the mouth, the brain, and the sensory organs, such as the eyes and the antennae, if there are any

**heart:** muscular tube that pumps blood

**incomplete metamorphosis:** a process of development in which the young look and behave much like a small adult except that they are unable to reproduce. Stages include egg, nymph, and adult.

**intestine (gut):** digestion is completed here. Food nutrients pass into the body cavity to enter the blood and flow to all body parts.

**larva:** the stage between egg and pupa in complete metamorphosis

**Malpighian** (mal-PEE-gee-an) **tubules:** the organ that cleans the blood and passes wastes to the intestine

**mandibles:** the grinding mouthparts of an insect

**molt:** the process of an insect shedding its exoskeleton

**nerve cord:** the nervous system. It sends messages between the brain and other body parts.

**nymph:** stage between egg and adult in incomplete metamorphosis

**ovary** (OH-vuh-ree)**:** body part that produces eggs

**ovipositor:** tail end of the abdomen used to deposit eggs

**pheromones** (FER-eh-mohnz)**:** chemical scents given off as a form of communication

**predator:** an animal that is a hunter

**prey:** an animal that a predator catches to eat

**pupa:** stage between larva and adult in complete metamorphosis. At this stage, the larva's body structure and systems are completely changed into its adult form.

**rectum:** part of digestive system where wastes collect before passing out of the body

**simple eyes:** eyes only able to sense light from dark

**sperm:** male reproductive cell

**spermatheca** (spur-muh-THEE-kuh)**:** sac in female insects that stores sperm after mating

**spiracles** (SPIR-i-kehlz)**:** holes down the sides of the thorax and abdomen. They let air into and out of the body for breathing.

**stomach:** the body part that receives food from the gizzard and continues digestion

**thorax:** the body part between the head and the abdomen

# DIGGING DEEPER

To keep on investigating stick insects, explore these books and websites.

## BOOKS

D'Agata, Tabatha Jean. *Ick the Stick*. Miami Beach: Bouncing Ball Books, 2006. Enjoy this easy-to-read story about a child's discovery of a stick insect.

Rompella, Natalie. *Don't Squash That Bug!: The Curious Kid's Guide to Insects*. Montreal: Lobster Press, 2007. Discover fun facts about insects of all kinds, including stick insects. Full-color photos add to the fun.

Watts, Barrie. *Stick Insects*. New York: Franklin Watts, 1992. Find out how to keep a stick insect as a pet. This how-to book shares facts about housing, feeding, and breeding stick insects.

## WEBSITES

**Leaf or Stick Insects**
http://www.kidcyber.com.au/topics/stickie.htm
This Australian website has photos and facts about leaf insects and stick insects. Follow the links to find out even more.

**San Diego Zoo: Stick Insects**
http://www.sandiegozoo.org/animalbytes/t-stick_insect.html
Check out fun facts and interesting information about the lives of stick insects.

**Walking Stick Insects: The Perfect Insect Pet**
http://www.biology.ualberta.ca/locke.hp/walk_sticks.htm
Find tips on the care and housing of a pet stick insect. Don't miss the experiments section.

# STICK INSECT ACTIVITIES

## HOST A STICK VISITOR

Stick insects are among the world's most popular insect pets. If you find a stick insect in your neighborhood, you could bring it home for a visit. At home, you would be able to watch it at night. That's when stick insects are most active. Just follow these steps to give your visitor a comfortable home. Then, after about a week, return the stick insect to its natural habitat.

1. Before you go looking for a stick insect, prepare a home for it. It will need a tall cage, one at least 18 inches (46 cm) high and nearly as wide. Stick insects need lots of air. A good stick insect home is made from a roll of window screen. Tie or tape the edges to make a tube. Set this tube in a shallow box. Top it with a piece of sturdy cardboard weighed down with a rock.

2. Line the bottom of the box with clean newspaper.

3. Use a pin to poke holes in a large, self-sealing plastic bag. Use this bag to carry home the stick insect you find.

4. In another plastic bag, bring home leaf-covered branches from the bush or tree where you find the insect. This will be the insect's food supply.

5. Place the branches and stick insect in its temporary home. Place the home in a warm spot, but not in direct sunlight.

6. Mist the plant (not the insect) with water every other day. Stick insects need to drink water, and they do this by drinking droplets on leaves.

7. Replace food branches when most leaves are gone or wilted.

## PLAY STICK INSECT TAG

Get a feel for the main way stick insects defend themselves from predators. To play, first choose someone to be the predator. Players who are the stick insects must keep moving until a predator comes toward them. Then they must freeze and stay perfectly still. This is the way a stick insect freezes to blend in and hide. If the game is played among trees, staying safe is touching a tree and being perfectly still. The first person to move is tagged out by the predator. The person tagged then takes a turn as the predator.

# INDEX

## PHOTO ACKNOWLEDGMENTS

The images in this book are used with the permission of: © Dwight R. Kuhn, pp. 4, 41 (middle and bottom); © PATRICIO ROBLES GIL/SIERRA MADRES/Minden Pictures, p. 5; © Michael & Patricia Fogden/CORBIS, pp. 6–7, 12; © Bill Hauser/Independent Picture Service, pp. 8–9; © Christian Ziegler, pp. 10 (both), 14, 25, 35, 37, 38–39; © Tony Jewell, p. 11, © Rod Williams/naturepl.com, p. 13; © NHPA/Anthony Bannister, p. 15; © FRANS LANTING/Minden Pictures, p. 17; © Anthony Bannister/CORBIS, p. 19; © Kazuo UNNO/Nature Production, p. 21; © Chris Mattison; Frank Lane Picture Agency/CORBIS, pp. 22–23; © E.R. DEGGINGER/Animals Animals, p. 27; © guichaoua/Alamy, pp. 28–29; © PETER MACDIARMID/Reuters/CORBIS, p. 31; Mike Merchant, Texas Cooperative Extension, p. 33; © REUTERS/handout, p. 41 (top); AP Photo/Idaho Press-Tribune, Greg Kreller, p. 46.

Front Cover: © Buddy Mays/CORBIS.